RELEVANT AND REVERENT

HUMAN LIKE ME, JESUS draws Christianity from behind Church doors into the everyday activities of home, school and street, closing the gap between divinity and daily life.

Malcolm Boyd penetrates the masks we wear to uncover the individuals we are in this extraordinary collection of personal meditations. He shares his thoughts and innermost feelings with all those who have ever felt lonely, lost, betrayed, bewildered. He brings us comfort, compassion and uncommon sense in this humane book for human beings everywhere.

HUMAN
LIKE ME,
JESUS

Malcolm Boyd

Revised and Abridged

With a New Introduction
to the Paperback Edition

PYRAMID FAMILY LIBRARY • NEW YORK

HUMAN LIKE ME, JESUS

A PYRAMID FAMILY LIBRARY BOOK
Published by arrangement with Simon and Schuster, Incorporated

Pyramid Family Library edition published December, 1973

ISBN 0-515-03107-0

Pyramid Family Library Books are published by Pyramid Communications, Inc. Its trademarks, consisting of the word "Pyramid" and the portrayal of a pyramid, are registered in the United States Patent Office.

PYRAMID COMMUNICATIONS, INC.
919 Third Avenue
New York, New York 10022, U.S.A.

TABLE OF CONTENTS

HUMAN LIKE ME, JESUS

INTRODUCTION

"Now I lay me down to sleep . . . ," I prayed as a child. Later I graduated to the Lord's Prayer.

I attended Sunday School regularly, served as an acolyte by the altar, and at one time sang in the choir.

The church occupied a central place in my young life. Many childhood memories revolve around it. I remember, on the evening when Orson Welles produced his classic radio broadcast about an imaginary Martian invasion of earth, that several friends and I attended a Sunday school supper at a cathedral.

Bored, we concocted a plan to climb up inside the stone tower after everybody had departed in order to ring the bells of the cathedral. We thought it had the makings of a lark.

After supper we separated ourselves from the rest of the people and patiently waited in a remote hall for them to go home. We would go about our business when we were locked snugly inside the cathedral. Finally distant lights were turned off, doors bolted, and voices drifted away into the night.

The radio program had begun its fateful broadcast—which would shortly result in national terror —when the four of us, alone inside the Gothic structure, moved swiftly through its dark interior. The splendid stained-glass windows appeared to be mere leaded spaces. The gigantic sanctuary with its stone altar seemed a treacherous inky expanse where evil spirits lurked ready to reach out with spiders' legs to pull us into a pit.

We found the door leading to the bell tower. The stairs were narrow and winding. We did not know what dead gargoyles or living church officials we might encounter face to face around the next turn of the stairs. Soon it became apparent we were being followed; I could hear the steady footsteps behind us. I told my companions to stop. We waited, holding our breath. The footsteps halted. We started again, tearing up the stairs, shouting at the top of our lungs to ward off evil spirits and confuse the demon in pursuit. We reached the bell tower, out of breath but ready to fight our pursuer. Only then did we realize the demon was our echo. We got down to the business of ringing the bells.

Unknown to us, the city was locked in deadly fear. To all intents and purposes, the Martians had landed. Switchboards of police stations, newspapers and broadcasting companies were swamped with desperate calls. Some people were in the streets, others had started out in their cars toward safety in the hills beyond the city.

Suddenly the bells of the cathedral boomed out their note of warning and possible death. Doom! Despair! Those who had held back in cynicism, rational behavior, or perhaps a growing edge of anxiety, leaped headlong (we learned afterward) into the cauldron of public discombobulation.

Alarm! Man the barricades! To the walls! Doors of private houses and apartment houses were thrust open as men, women and children rushed into the night air. They looked toward the fortress of Almighty God, the Gothic stone pile of the cathedral, seeking reassurance or any sign of divine will. The cathedral presented the same face as always, betraying no evidence of God's intervention in men's affairs except for the fact that its mighty bell tower shook—heaved!—with the growing splendor of the clashing night bells ringing out over humanity in disarray. Elderly women fell to their knees in prayer. Men crossed themselves. Rosaries were in evidence. Tears streamed down faces.

Soon word started reaching the people that there *were* no Martians. The best thing to do was go home and get to sleep. Breathless with excitement about our achievement of ringing the bells, the four of us were now making our way down the winding stairway when we heard the ominous sound of police sirens. We realized that they were coming for us. Wondering if ringing the bells had been a major civic offense, and totally without knowledge of what had transpired outside in the city that night, we raced into the cathedral sanctuary mere footsteps ahead of a small army of police.

As I crouched behind the bishop's throne in the shadows, it seemed to me that church and state were not adequately separated. When the police made their way up the stairway to the bell tower we fled through a convenient herb garden of the cathedral toward our homes.

My childhood knowledge about God came partly from occasional but memorably majestic invocations and benedictions delivered in a loud voice at school assemblies by clerics garbed in deathly black.

Little did I know, at that time, that I would later enter a theological seminary, become ordained as an Episcopal priest, and serve in the church during a period of stark revolutionary change.

The church is always healthier when it is responding, in genuine crisis and controversy, to honest tensions in the life of the world. I recall a bishop saying, "I have two types of clergy in my diocese, the disturbed and the dead. I hope that I will remain always one of the disturbed." A number of disturbed clergy and laymen are moving close together in a new life style that disrupts the old caste system separating them.

An alive church will increasingly find its altar out on Main Street, its holiest people ordinary men and women who care about other people (and so, about God), and its "social action" placing its own body on the line, inseparable from the love it is always talking about in pulpits. A public demonstration is a good thing to jar a pickled conscience. But really effective social action (obedience to the gospel) is ongoing, steady, localized work rooted in such realities as "salvation" of education, housing, jobs, peace, politics and breaking down ghetto walls.

On the one hand, the establishment church is the locus of those Sunday newspaper society wedding accounts; this a part of its being the place where the establishment marries, baptizes and buries, but virtually never conceives. On the other hand, the essential church is the continuing movement that shattered the peace of a Peter, a Paul, a Francis, a Luther, a Kierkegaard, a Unamuno, a Marx and a Hammarskjöld. Success seems to be coming to the church. Not by publicity-measured real-estate construction, vaulted cathedrals, or power structure prelates and evangelists who are "in" with the government and politicians.

The success symbol of sacrifice and brotherhood becomes ever more central to the experience of haunted contemporary men and women who seek self-possession amid the accouterments of affluence, a sign of personal identity in the cloverleaf of technology, and communion with other people instead of coexistence with posthumans who have been tranlated into machines.

At this crucial moment religious complacency is a buried fantasy. The essential church—pockets of pilgrims who have communion with each other in

dispersion, and experience heightened hope in sadness—comprehends that it must be ready to die, in
this generation, celebrating new life in the person
of the Jesus whom it calls lord and brother. Even
the militant, activist, sometimes frightening reform-
ers—invariably seen as cultural anti-heroes—are
caught in an anguished fear they seldom communicate to sophisticated newsmen and impersonal TV
cameras. Their fear is that they may be acting out
of "self-righteousness," which has replaced "pater-
nalism" as the current most damning word.

All in all—and despite bloodstains, wasteland
rhetoric and racking strains that shatter lives—the
essential church is passionately alive, embarrass-
ingly well (in light, that is, of various seers' prog-
nostications about its demise) and living in a moon-
drenched world of sensitive, crazy, changing and
growing people. These people do not hear the majestic, traditionally martial strains celebrating the
divine Hero in regally imperial glory and establishment power. Instead there is quiet celebration of
the life, death and resurrection of Jesus, the anti-
hero of his own time, the brother and servant who
died on the cross in God's identification with human
injustice, suffering, failure and hope.

Human Like Me, Jesus is an affirmation of three
beliefs that are central to my life.

The first belief is that the humanness I share
with other people links us together with an iron
strength that stands against all separation, all
ghettos, any apartheid.

The second belief is that my own humanness can
never be taken away from me, either by a form of
dehumanization seeking to crush me, or by tragic
expressions of anti-life taking root within my own
occasional feelings of anxiety and despair.

The third belief is that Jesus shares a common

bond of humanity with all other people and myself.
So Jesus illumines human life with holiness, rendering indissoluble what we call "the sacred" and "the secular."

Although some people hate organized religion or are indifferent to it, they do not (I strongly believe) hate prayer or utterly shun what it implies—another dimension of life. Most people are open to an awareness of mystery, sacrifice and celebration.

Prayer exists even when it is not called prayer or uttered or even acknowledged.

MALCOLM BOYD

May 26, 1973

HUMAN LIKE ME, JESUS

PRAYERS

OF PERSONAL

IDENTITY

Who am I, Jesus?

I know there is a face, a smile, and a frown. There is passion, a residue of rage, and an icy capacity to withdraw. There is the familiar body, the uncharted mind, and the chameleon performing as a clown.

I know there is a tenderness, a warmth, and a biting revenge that reacts to real or imaginary hurt. There is the man-woman, the child, and the indelible image of God that calls to me in what I know as a conscience. There is a hunger that is insatiable, a thirst that burns and gnaws, and a hard selfishness that can be viciously cruel.

I know there is a vaulting ambition, a complex drive that will not let me rest, and a laziness made for a summer's day. There is an idealism that can startle my self-interest, a sense of duty that can suffocate my ticklish inclinations toward abandon, and a ruthless sense of self-sovereignty that can arrogantly try to bluff even Almighty God.

I know there is a cultivated self-sufficiency, a suicidal loneliness, and a dreaded anxiety. There is a personal history with tears and laughter, a public life, and a being so vulnerable that it can be smashed into pieces like a glass.

What is there in me of holiness, Jesus? What is there within me possessing hidden life that cannot be broken or burned or obliterated? What is there of me that is love, Lord?

You became human, Jesus. As a man you experienced loneliness, anger, joy, depression and hope.

Thank you for being human like me, Jesus.

I remember one night when I was a child, Jesus.

The soft light in the hallway seemed to flicker.
There were footsteps on the stairs. My heart pound-
ed. The footsteps were heavy—one, two, one, two.
They came to the head of the stairs outside my
room. It was the stout woman who had been hired
to stay with me while my parents went out to the
theater.

I was afraid of her. I knew that she did not like
me. She treated me kindly when my parents were
with us, but showed a cold hostility when we were
alone. What did she want? Now the sound of footsteps ended. The silence was distressing. I must act
as if I were asleep. I dared not move my eyelids or
any part of my body. My back itched. My left leg
felt as if it had a cramp.

The footsteps began again, creaking on the floor
as they approached my bed. The stout woman
stood by the side of the bed. I wanted to cry out,
leap from my sheets and blankets, and run toward
the door, but I knew it would be of no use. She
would catch me. She must be looking down at my
body in the long silence. Was she going to cook me
in a great stew and eat me? She would tell my father and mother, when they came home, that I had
run away. They would believe her and the terrible
injustice would stand. No. No. Don't let her do
this to me. I heard her footsteps on the bedroom
floor. She was going away. She had decided not to
cook me now but wait until later. Her footsteps
were going down the stairs.

I must have fallen asleep. Suddenly, as if they
had just begun speaking, two voices broke into my

hearing. They were angry. I listened harder. They belonged to my father and mother. I almost jumped out of my bed to run into their room. I was happy that they had come home. The stout woman must have gone away. I was safe again.

But the anger in their voices warned me. I lay still in my bed, listening. I could not hear what words they were saying to each other. Then my mother said that she could not stand it any longer. My father swore at her. I heard a crash. What had happened? Was one of them hurt? I heard a door slam, and there was silence in the next room except for my mother's crying. The next morning I saw what had crashed. It was the glass covering a photograph of my father that always stood on their dresser.

All the next day the mood in the house was ominous. No one talked. I was treated as a child who did not know what had happened. That night my father and mother talked to me at the dinner table. They were going to separate, my mother said. That meant they would not live together anymore. My father took me up on his lap to hold me. He said they both wanted me to be happy. Would I decide which one of them I wanted to live with?

The next day, running in the ocean waves at the beach, with the sand between my toes, in my eyes and mouth, I felt that my heart had closed in on itself.

How much can a child understand, Jesus?

What is effectiveness, Jesus?

Some people place it ahead of honesty. But without honesty, wouldn't something just appear on the surface to be effective? I mean, it would really be a failure, Lord.

Success and failure seem to be badly misunderstood, don't they? They are judged by outward appearances instead of inner realities. I have felt my deepest failure at moments when people said I was a success, Lord. I have felt fulfilled and successful as a human being when I was most severely judged to be a failure.

You have taught us, Jesus, that a person can gain the whole world and lose his soul. This seems to be true for whole nations and societies too. Have we ever really heard what you were saying, Lord?

I envy someone, Jesus.

He is also someone whom I respect. It is just that he seems to be a better person than I am. He is gifted, kind, compassionate, patient and much more productive than I. He receives public acclaim in a situation where I have done as much work and am not thanked at all.

Why can't I accept his superiority gracefully, Lord? Why do I engage in this unprofitable and mean exercise of making comparisons between myself and him?

The feeling of envy cuts into my soul like acid eating flesh. I am burning and writhing under the pain, Jesus. The very existence of this person has become an irrational and insatiable threat to my being. Why am I so weak? Why am I so evil?

Help me to love the person whom I envy, Lord. Help me to love myself.

I was playing hopscotch around the center core of my life, Lord.

And before I knew it, I was consuming alcohol with the fervor of an addict. I set out to extinguish my fires, but they burned all the more brightly. I attended jet-set parties where waiters handed everybody a lethal new Martini, swimming luxuriantly in a clear glass, every eight minutes. I counted, Jesus.

I drank in neighborhood bars, those chummy, intimate, subdued places where quiet manners obscured the alcoholic brew that was churning inside their patrons' stomachs and heads.

At parties my friends gave I drank past the danger mark until I discovered that I had angrily broken a glass or accusingly insulted a fellow guest. Nice party, Sally! Great time, Danny! I stopped, Lord. Oh, I still take a drink, but I am not putting out fires. I have learned that fire is only fire.

Thanks for helping me to look deeply into that center core of my life, Jesus. Thanks for helping me to accept myself.

I feel detached from myself right now, Jesus.

It seems there are maybe four parts of me, or twelve, or thirty. Am I a simple schizoid or a whole complex pattern?

Someone asked me how I live with loneliness, Lord. Lone-li-ness. It seemed to me the alternative would be to die with it.

In this moment I am here, and there, and over *there*, and back *here*. I am interestingly fragmented, Jesus. I am in the present, the past, and the future. I am yellow and red and white and black and brown. I am Chinese in the thirteenth century, San Franciscan in the twenty-second, and Hun in the sixth. I am Babylonian. I am Assyrian. I am Chicagoan. I am Parisian. The human experience is splendid fun today, Jesus.

Once I thought that I should be a hero, Jesus.

Advancing against the enemy on a warrior's charger, with a mighty sword in my hand, I would uphold purity and justice against decadence and tyranny.

If a mere person lurked inside my hero's image, he must be denied, disciplined—flogged into submission, if need be—and forgotten. As a hero I realized that I would be lonely, Lord, even in the midst of convivial community, for I knew that I could never relax my role.

I could be king or president, messiah or bishop, general or statesman; they were heroes.

Then, one day, Jesus, I realized that I did not want to be a hero.

I cannot comprehend death, Jesus.

Will I be alive one moment, with all the submarine mechanism working, valves grinding, doors inside opening and closing—my dreams and hopes, plans and memories, fully charged with energy—and then, the next moment, will it all stop?

I don't know if I want to die or not, Lord.

Is life after death livable? I wonder if the intellect is respected, the arts flourish, there is at least a modicum of political integrity, and people love one another.

It scares me sometimes to be very serious about death, Lord. I would like to laugh about it too. Jesus, help me to understand what it is all about.

I have masqueraded as many things, Jesus.

Wasn't it easier, when I stepped outside the front door of my house, to meet the needs of others by becoming what they wished me to be? I was sad, I was gay. I listened attentively, I spoke in words of wisdom. I was humble and dutiful, I was proud and commanding. I asked myself, Doesn't love require this?

All of us have played roles for such a long time. Yet we are humans, Lord. If we did not so fiercely hold to our roles, and obstinately imprison each other inside them, we might learn to understand each other. Do you feel we might even learn how to be compassionate, Jesus?

The inky prophecies of today's newspaper are gloomy, Jesus.

But I don't want to be dismayed by what appears hard or even hopeless.

I want to celebrate life.

Blood flows through my veins. Rain falls, Lord. Waters surge through the earth.

I know that the sun is up, Jesus, even when it is hidden by low gray clouds.

I know that the wind is here, even when it is so still. Look! A leaf trembles on that tree.

I can see yellows, reds, blues, greens, black and white.

Love. It is all around me. Sometimes it is called hate.

I feel like singing, smelling, looking, biting, laughing, tasting, crying, painting, walking, dancing, running . . .

Living, Jesus.

PEOPLE

It was a swinging party, Jesus.

But the people seemed to be tense. They were in constant motion and playing tight roles. Everybody was scripted and choreographed. Booze covered up a multitude of neuroses. Celebration! Everybody was to have fun!

I saw a woman dressed in gold pajamas and enough costume jewelry to sink an excursion boat. She had had too much to drink. She kept saying, "I want to work with the poor in Africa. ... The poor ... Africa ... I want to work with the poor in Africa."

I wondered what she really wanted, Lord, and what was her Africa.

A heavy frame separates me from the bearded man in the painting, Jesus.

Does it provide him with an illusion of noninvolvement?

He is yawning. Now he begins coming through to me as someone trying to play a smug role. He is not succeeding, for I see through his painted outer mask of charming dilettantism and exaggerated ease.

The man painted in oils inside the frame that separates us is not relaxed at all, Lord. Neither am I. We need to talk.

I would like to throw away all frames.

He doesn't know how his children are going to eat tonight, Jesus.

There is just no money left. He has tried everything but cannot find a job. His wife is sick and doesn't have the right kind of care.

His little girl is crying. The sound of it is a bit louder than the dialogue of an old movie that is playing on the TV set. His boys are sitting huddled on an old sofa, watching the images flicker on the television screen.

Lord, he wishes that he knew what to do.

She is outwardly a very, very correct woman, Jesus.

But her interior life is in disarray. She suspects that she may be having a long and continuous nervous breakdown.

It isn't that she can't function, Lord. She goes through all the motions excellently. However, she hasn't even the vaguest idea of what she truly believes about anything. Her identity is a remote face that she looks at in the mirror of a morning, adding a touch of rouge here, a bit of powder there, and now contemplating a pleasant smile, perfect white teeth, and a hint of mystery within the eyes.

She is searching for a handy kind of magic glue, Lord, to hold together lots of broken pieces that comprise what is known as her life: car keys, office-door keys, desk keys, apartment keys, a social security number, pills, photographs, telephone numbers, credit cards, a jigger of fear, a dash of loneliness, and she has to hurry now.

Can she connect the outside of her life with the inside of it, Jesus?

She is in high school, Jesus.

While she was growing up, social issues held the center of the stages of her life. There was talk about freedom, which many different people felt they had been denied. This made her wonder about her own freedom, Lord.

"I've become free all around," she said, her face breaking into a happy grin.

"Through the teaching of freedom by close friends and Gibran and Gandhi and Diogenes and others. I realized my freedom through the words of my sociology teacher in our high school. A surprise package came with my freedom, if being freer weren't enough, but I am more and more becoming and *being* nonviolent. This is a very important thing to me."

Her eyes search the ground and the sky outside the big window alongside us.

"You know what I've discovered—realized—through others' realizations? That I am unable to love. To love one single person in a romantic boy-girl relationship. That people, my age especially, think love is a cow when it's really an elephant. They're always believing an elephant is a cow—and no wonder there are so many divorces when people marry merely for love.

"So now that I realize that I can't love and won't be able to love for quite a while—well, no sweat. I can be freer. All of which does not mean that I can act and react lovingly. And when I *know* that I don't know what love is, I can't be hurt by it. Lord, I'm a kite!"

Help her to share her freedom, Jesus.

Everywhere I see color, Lord.

A brown man wearing a red shirt, blue coat, checkered vest and striped pants is walking across a yellow bridge in the park. Surrounding trees are green. Beneath the bridge the water is silver. The sky is trumpet-blue.

Where is the man in the colored world going, Jesus?

Today she is seventy years old, Lord.

Everybody else is concerned about her birthday celebration while she is cooking breakfast and planning a visit to the grocery store.

It doesn't seem possible to her that she is seventy. Where did the years go? Her interests and thoughts are very young ones, moving backward swiftly over many years.

Where did the last week go so quickly? The last day—the last hour? Time is running through a sieve.

But, of course, she is not bound by it. She is free. Fear is merely a word. She sees her mother and father. Remember the picnic when she turned ten years old? She sees her college roommate and her Latin teacher and her husband and her baby and . . .

Somebody is telephoning to wish her a happy birthday.

She doesn't understand why nobody seems to realize how young she really is, Jesus.

PRAYERS

FOR SEXUAL

HUMANNESS

How do loving and liking relate, Lord?

He is forty-five, professionally successful and socially integrated into several groups of interesting people. He likes to have sex with a lot of women, but is desperately afraid of loving them. It is love that he is afraid of. It might open up his life, and then the barriers constructed around his vulnerability could fall down.

So he plays the tough guy with machismo, the laughing man, the big spender and the cynic. When all these roles come together, they lay a heavy weight on a highly insecure, man-sized boy who is afraid to grow up. Not only are women objects to him but he remains an object to himself.

He's telling another story, Jesus. People around him are laughing. He is strutting, building his yarn to its climax—a middle-aged kid with his slingshot.

Can he find that love is childlike instead of childish, Jesus?

"I'm tired of one-night stands," the young woman told me, Jesus.

She has heard all the theories about how smart it would be to wait until she is past thirty before getting married, Jesus, and she doesn't agree.

The young woman is very pretty, with dark, luminous eyes and black hair combed straight back. She works as a secretary in an office.

"Not many guys who take me out want any emotional involvement," she said. "The minute I say that I care, it's split—out the door, out the window. They don't want to get into feelings."

She smiled sadly.

"I want to get married and have kids. But I don't see this happening to me. Not with any of the guys I know. Not if I stay here. Not if I go on living as I've been doing. But what else can I do? It scares me. If I try to change, I know that I'll find out how many things in life now aren't real for me."

How can she handle realities in her life, Jesus? Will she be able to live with feelings and emotions in the open?

He doesn't know if he is afraid of sex or not, Jesus.

He is thirty-five, good-looking, active in public life, and homosexual. He found out, or finally accepted the fact, that he was gay before a brief and sad marriage terminated.

So he went through the gay bars like a house afire. He had a lot of sex with a lot of partners. He learned many tricks, swung with a hip style, accepted his new happiness, and then one day realized that he didn't want raw sex anymore without someone to love.

But this meant an open social acceptance of his homosexuality. He didn't want to define himself that way. Wasn't he human first of all? Yet society would deny that. A whole identity crisis, to be lived in public, confronted him.

He continues looking for the man with whom he can share love, working against the pressures that would confine him to sex without love or life without the kind of fulfilling sex that he seeks.

Can his fears be resolved, Jesus?

How can people free rather than imprison each other in relationship, Lord?

This is the question she asks every time she meets a new man in whom she might be interested.

She got a divorce six months ago. As a matter of fact, she still loves her former husband. She admits that love and hate are close. But she couldn't live with him anymore. Life with him became claustrophobic. She wonders if perhaps she married him too early, before she had more sexual experiences. Anyhow, she saw it through. The kids are grown and in college.

She's free. However, she's lonely in the mornings, the late afternoons and at night. She drinks too much. She isn't sure whom she should sleep with, but she has learned that a lot of sexual advances are made to a divorcee, especially by her former husband's best friends.

She wants a relationship with a man to free her from the prison of her loneliness and self-destruction, Lord. But she wonders if relationship itself ever means freedom.

What is sex, Jesus?

He was taught that it meant the sex act. His instruction took place in the basement of a neighboring house several years ago when some older boys decided to share the facts of life with him. His mother and father never did. His school never did.

Now he is a high-school student. He has begun to realize that sex seems to be a part of breathing, looking, touching, thinking and living. Yet he knows it is also a precise act at a particular time. He has experienced that act with a girl. He has masturbated.

None of this makes him feel at all disturbed except for the fact that a lot of people probably say he shouldn't have done these things. He wonders why.

He expects to be living his life with his sex drive for a long time. He would like to avoid hang-ups. He would rather not hurt anyone else because of sex. He wishes there could be more openness and less hypocrisy about something that seems to be so essential in everybody's life. He has talked with friends recently about the possibility of one day having a vasectomy so that he won't contribute to bringing too many children into the world.

Sex seems nice as well as a somewhat complicated thing to him, Jesus.

She was telling me about her search for love, Lord.

The young woman, a high-school graduate who works in a suburban office, met a man and went to bed with him. He was not the first.

"We bumped into each other, literally, and he kissed me. I was on my coffee break, he was passing through the building. We talked for a while and I agreed to a rendezvous. I said I didn't want another love thing. He said he was married and had two children.

"I began to see Frank for an hour here and there. About two months later we were in love. Frank was sick about it. He didn't want it any more than I did. I didn't think about anything when I was with him. Just us. We talked so very much. More than we made love, even.

"Through all this I was pregnant with another man's child. That was a one-way, sex-for-love relationship. I had needed love but took sex instead, hoping Ralph might begin to love me if I pleased him. When I told him I was bearing his child he could have killed me. After the things he said I did die partially.

"And that was that. Don't bother him anymore about it. Ever. I wanted my baby so very much. But without a father, without anyone in the world except me, and me without money, she couldn't have had a chance. She was adopted by a young couple.

"My baby was so beautiful. I held her in my arms before I gave her over. She looked at me so angrily. But she'll learn someday how much I had to love her to give her up. Every time I think of her I cry, as I'm doing now.

"Now it's many months since I had her. I had to quit my job because the strain was so great. I've only spoken to Frank a few times, briefly. We want to see each other often again. Conditions aren't right yet, but they probably will be soon. Regardless of the way I am, I'm me, and that's all there is."

Lord, I couldn't help wondering how long she would try to cover up her loneliness. Can she find the love that she is looking for, Jesus?

What can marriage mean, Jesus?

They wonder once again, but now it is a little
late to ask. The church is decorated with candles to
provide light for their evening wedding.

Their parents are up front. Guests, including lots
of school friends, have crowded into the Gothic
structure. A former roommate of his is playing gui-
tar music softly. A former roommate of hers will
read a poem.

The minister will say "... to have and to hold
from this day forward, for better for worse, for
richer for poorer, in sickness and in health, to love
and to cherish, till death us do part ..."

They feel separate from each other, as they
haven't in months. For one thing, they haven't
slept together during the past week, since they've
both been living in their old homes again. Too,
they are anxious about this public proclamation of
themselves. They hope it will not bruise something
sensitive and private in their love, Lord.

The procession is moving up the aisle, Jesus.

What does it mean to create a baby, Lord?

They're married and asking themselves the question. It frightens them, Jesus.

They don't want to program another human life. They don't want to be stuck with authority roles that they have come to question in experiences with their parents. And they are not sure that they will remain married, for they question permanent monogamy and the strength of the family as an institution.

They have thought of becoming part of a commune. A baby would grow up inside a commune with a number of different parental figures. But, it occurs to them, the commune experience might be as temporary as their marriage.

They want to know, Lord, what a baby would really mean in their own lives and as a new human being in life itself.

She used to be too boldly aggressive about sex, Lord.

That is what her family and friends led her to believe. One close friend asked over drinks once if she was a nymphomaniac.

This led her into a long period when she has repressed her feelings. She was ashamed of the passion and joy she experienced in making love. She grew wary of her image as a fun-loving and warm woman. Her husband never seemed to understand her passion, for he wished to place his wife on a kind of pedestal. However, when she denied full expression to her sexual feelings, he proceeded to have an affair with another woman.

The question of how natural one should feel about sex has plagued her ever since. Should someone civilized, particularly a woman, tame or deny natural sexual instincts and instead play a programmed role even in bed with her husband? It is the question she asks. It seems to deeply affect her humanness.

Can she accept sex as a natural part of her life, Jesus, and also find acceptance in that naturalness?

Prayer for two people being married.

Bless Barbara and Richard, Lord.

Bless them with deep understanding and warm companionship.

Bless them with a love that grows.

Bless them with a concern for others that is nourished by their mutual concern.

Bless them with patience and urgency, commitment and relaxation, involvement in all of life and peace as your gift.

Bless them with gentleness and serenity.

Bless all those whom they love and who love them.

Bless Richard and Barbara, Lord.

They have been in love for forty years, Lord.

They will be the first to say that it wasn't all a bed of roses. They accepted their marriage as the most important fact in their lives, so they simply spent more time and energy on it than on anything else.

Of course, this meant not spending time and energy on each other beyond a point. Instead they got involved, often separately, with a lot of other people and their concerns.

Humor has helped them a lot. The discipline of getting on with it in place of wondering whether they ought to or not. Listening as well as speaking. A healthy development of sexual fantasy to let sex remain exciting, not become routine. And unrelenting awareness of how stiflingly boring boredom can be.

They give a lot of love to life, Jesus.

PRAYERS

IN THE

SEASONS

I feel a dead leaf on the weathered branch of a black tree, Jesus.

Between my fingers it is like crisp parchment.

The wind blows steadily on this early April afternoon as I walk through a cemetery.

A graying tombstone announces:

JOHN G   1829-1862
His Wife
JUDITH ANN   1835-1909
Daughter
NANCY MARGARET   1859-1937.

An immense brown monument contains a single name, Esher, and a gigantic cross. Two orange flowerpots, one empty, the other half-filled with dirt, are overturned beneath it in the dancing shadow of moving paper leaves.

There, in the distance, a small green pine indicates life. An American flag waves in the wind, over there to the left, in front of a headstone. A wreath of dead flowers with a large, dirty red bow marks a tomb directly in front of me.

I am walking over the dead. Their flesh has vanished. I suppose their bones remain. I do not wish to dishonor them by treading them underfoot. It is the spring earth I seek communion with.

WIFE OF THOMAS PHIPPS
DIED 1893
AGED
48 YRS. 6 MO.
REST IN PEACE.

An angel—How did I know?—this baby figure
with immense wings, carved out of stone, is blowing
a trumpet over a grave to my left. A car drives into
the cemetery and moves slowly past me. Two
women stop for a moment, not getting out of the
car. They look silently toward a grave. Then they
drive on, around the sloping road and outside
again. The wind is noisy today. A small bird, flying
over me through gaunt branches, chirps simple, un-
pretty notes.

I am startled to find that I have almost walked
on a piece of ice (Why hasn't it melted?), the sole
remnant of the winter's last snowstorm a week ago.
A fly zooms in front of me, smelling me before
pirouetting away.

MOTHER
ANNE

An urn of artificial flowers appears now on my left. A sacrificial lamb is carved atop a tombstone bearing the name Lucia. A wooden, suffering, thorn-crowned Christ is crucified over a tombstone nearby, surrounded by small pine trees.

MY-SELF proclaims one small tombstone. The sunlight catches the surface of a distant stone, making it shine like a windowpane. A six-year-old boy was buried *here;* a tiny cement angel bearing a cross recalls him. Ashes to ashes. "A Native of Ireland" says a stone *there.* Dust to dust. Passion lurks in dust. There is a heartbeat in ashes. Who can define ashes? Who can label dust? I walk through the shadow cast by a large white angel, its hands lifted high.

I do not feel sad, Lord. I am peaceful and resting here, catching my breath, alive for a moment amid the death of life outside: car fumes, the drone of television, people rushing to keep pace with machines, racism, war, and encroaching rage. Jesus, this seems to be one of the few quietly reflective places left in the world. Lord, I am grateful to be alive.

It is raining on a summer afternoon, Jesus.

I am looking through a cardboard box of old letters and photographs in the attic. The sound of the falling rain on the wooden roof is gentle, Lord.

Here, handwritten by my grandmother, who died many years ago, is a recipe for jelly roll. 3 eggs. ½ cup sugar. ⅔ cup flour. ¾ tsp. baking powder. Butter a shallow pan. Bake in a quick oven.

Michael's letter before he committed suicide at Oxford. Postcards Jean sent from the Greek Islands the summer she visited there.

The last letter I received from my father before he died. His writing is wobbly, not so firm as it was before his illness. "I love you dearly, son."

The whole world, do you have it in your hands, Lord?

It was autumn, Jesus.

I was in my old house, set back from the road among tall trees. It had been sold, and I would have to depart the next morning so that the new owners could move in.

On that last night I sat late by the hearth. The flames of a roaring fire illuminated the red bricks of the grate and the dull bronze andirons. Sparks flew with abandon up the chimney, and I thought the roof of the house, with its pile of banked dead leaves, would surely catch fire.

It had seemed at first that the great log would not burn. It sputtered mildly. I rolled up more newspaper pages into balls and placed them strategically, with kindling wood underneath and around the log. Finally it caught, crackling with unabashed zest and immense exuberance; but it took hours to burn out.

At the end there were just blazing-hot, ruby-red coals on the floor of the hearth, sending light and heat into the cold—and, I am convinced, haunted—room, making weaving shadows play like friendly ghosts on the ceiling and walls. I sat looking at the fire. An hour passed, then another. I could not persuade myself to go. I would not be able to sit again before this hearth, warming myself and dreaming, communing with the past of this lovely and gracious house.

I slept there before the hearth that night. My emotions were dry and stored away the next morning when I departed. But why did I have to leave? Why do we let life do things to us, Jesus? Aren't we in charge, Lord?

We are the people who rule the earth, they say. Machines exist only to serve us. Life is a mechanism, an experience, under our control. If I was meant to have dominion over animals and machines and time and the exigencies of life, why am I not the ruler? But, Jesus, I am a slave. Is it enslavement to forces inside or outside myself, Lord?

Jesus, I do not want to be the ruler, but I do want to be free.

I am looking through a window, Lord, at snow and ice on the ground outside.

Suddenly a small rabbit darts across my line of vision. It pauses, trembling, beside a frozen bush. Now it runs across an exposed patch of ground, stopping beneath a tree. I can scarcely discern its body in the dark shadows.

The rabbit lives in the grip of death. So do I, Jesus. The purity of air and water concern him as much as me. A nuclear war or accident would destroy us both. His tiny gray body and mine—larger, differently formed—are vulnerable together on the face of the earth, Lord.

If people want to destroy themselves, Jesus, they should take a vote among the animals, the flowers and the trees. Any decision to die should be a democratic one.

The snow is falling, Jesus.

PRAYERS
ON CURIOUS
OCCASIONS

I had to say goodbye, Jesus.

The entire incident could now no longer be saved from tears, the whip of fleeting final moments upon tenderness, and the absolute and perhaps merciful blurring of reality.

Then it was done. Goodbye had been said. A door closed. A motor started and disappeared into the distance. My heart that had cracked loudly into many pieces now stopped beating altogether.

Jesus, please share my aloneness. Here, I give it to you, Lord. Please take it, Christ.

It was May Day at a country fair, Jesus.

I found myself in the midst of a slow-moving crowd of people, families with small children carried on their fathers' shoulders, boys and girls barefoot, and elderly people carrying paper bags filled with fresh turnips, onions and squash.

White Baby's Breath was for sale at Stall No. 24. I saw a hand-lettered sign directly in front of me bearing the words *Bleeding Heart. Blooms All Summer.*

A young friend of mine, a six-year-old boy, found hundreds of polliwogs in a water-filled ditch just outside the fair grounds and scooped up one of them in a paper cup. Then, his conscience bothering him, he returned the polliwog to approximately the same spot in the ditch from which it had been taken.

First Ayd said one of the signs outside the Renaissance Pleasure Faire. We were inside the fair grounds now. Four madrigal singers were entertaining a dozen attentive people. Nearly everybody was attired in medieval costume. I had retrieved a bright blue fourteenth-century French chasuble from a trunk where I had long ago packed it away. I wore it, with a matching stole, over an open-necked plain shirt and Levi's. Men and women danced on the green, and hawkers were selling clay flutes. Dogs of all sizes and descriptions were everywhere underfoot. People on horseback rode through the crowd. Signs pointed out *Glassmakers Lane, Potter's Market, Printmakers Way* and *Candlemakers' Cove.* Mead and ale, Cornish pasties, meat pies, popovers, tarts and fyne roasted chycken were available at stalls.

Cameos of Renaissance Drama Including "The Taming of the Shrew" led off the day's bill at the theater. Musical interludes were provided by an Italian Renaissance consort of ancient instruments.

"It's organic—it grows," someone said. "We've tried to reproduce what would actually be at a Renaissance fair. So we have included the Viking heritage, North Africa and, for example, spices that traders in Europe would have brought back from the Orient. The Renaissance fair was a comprehensive world, like the court of that time. One found mixed stations, different backgrounds, as people simply mingled together. Villages were too small to have anything but inns, and markets could be found only at the fairs."

I chatted with several new friends. One said that a witch had cast a fertility spell over his house. His wife was pregnant. All the flowers were blooming. Even the cat was having kittens.

A black goat wearing a straw hat ambled by. A tumbling act had concluded, a belly dancer was about to begin. Then she would be followed by a folk singer offering sixteenth-century songs. A sign announced a stall's name, *Earth Mother*. Someone asked me for help. "I'm looking for the Golden Toad, who is the next performer on the stage," she said.

I talked with a student. "Everybody at the fair just gets together and falls into the same mood," he told me. "There's a comfort in being with people you don't know who share the same attitudes and feelings as you do. And it's great to have that happen out in the country on a nice day. The clothes people wear, the colors, the excitement—all this is great. People put on these costumes and become all the exciting people they've always wanted to be. Everybody can do it. There aren't any limits. People can wear flowers in their hair if they want to. People don't have to wear flowers in their hair if they don't want to. It's beautiful."

I burned my mouth eating a hot fruit tart. I drank ginger beer. Someone in the distance was flying a kite. People milled around or sat on bundles of hay observing others. Flags and banners of yellow, orange, blue and red were matched by the colors in people's clothing. A pretty girl offered me a bite of French bread and cheese. The rolling hills and green slopes eased gently down to streams of water where kids were wading. The old trees seemed to be out of Sherwood Forest.

"You walk down most city streets in a costume and you frighten people," someone was saying. "It's sad that people are so jumpy and scared. Here it's a comfortable atmosphere."

Jesus, we need more country fairs, don't we?

Tension had been building to a showdown in our group, Jesus.

I knew my raw nerves were exposed. I had a sudden, vivid awareness that my reserve of patience and energy was all used up. Apparently the others felt the same way.

Everything blew up, Lord. We sat there afterward in silence amid the awful shambles of what we had done to each other. We were frightened and ashamed of being psychically stark naked in front of each other.

There were no recriminations or ritualistic acts of self-justification. But we dug at roots and new beginnings. Feelers were extended gently. Ideas were unraveled. Suddenly it became evident that the incident of violence would hold no explicit reference for us beyond itself.

Most unexpectedly, we all shared a healing experience. Healing can be a funny thing, can't it, Lord?

Mike, my dog, was dying on that rainy day.

"Man" and "Dog." I had often wondered about the relationship between Mike and the human world. How had he looked at life, houses, shops from a speeding car, lights in tall buildings at night, authority and freedom, the human schedule he had grown accustomed to, squirrels and cats—and me?

Mike, who was sixteen years old, somehow got to his feet and stood beside me. I reached out to touch the head and body of a close companion before he died.

How can I understand the mystery of the relationship between animals and humans, Lord?

I have a fever, Jesus.

It paralyzes my senses. I don't have the will or strength to get out of bed. I can scarcely turn my body over. All I seem to want right now is oblivion.

The fever is like an electric current moving behind my eyes and in my limbs. I need to feel cool. Just lying here in bed, scarcely breathing, without making any physical exertion at all, is the closest I can come to feeling cool. I have a capacity for sleep like a blotter for ink.

I took health for granted, didn't I, Lord? Please be master of the fever, Jesus.

It was a curious happening, Jesus.

In the eyes of a tired businessman who watched a long column of college men and women march in front of his car on a downtown city street, the event probably seemed to be an angry, maybe dangerous, student demonstration. Yet, in contrast with such imagery, the occasion was poignant for the youths' helplessness and the gentleness of their sober intensity in the face of a moral outrage.

An hour earlier the plaza on the campus was cold beneath the wind that had a late-winter ferocity. A number of us stood around a makeshift platform. Guerrilla theater players attired in military dress, juxtaposed against policemen in attendance, established a bizarre illusion of a police state.

A mock coffin, draped in black crepe paper, lay on the platform. It bore the name of Pvt. Richard Bunch. Two students, a man and a woman, stood on the platform holding a large banner that read *Free the Presidio 27*. The crowd was composed almost entirely of students, with only a sprinkling of faculty members.

Pvt. Richard Bunch had been shotgunned to death by a guard at the Presidio Military Prison in San Francisco, it was explained to us by a graduate student. He told how twenty-seven other prisoners, protesting the killing of Bunch as well as their own dehumanizing conditions inside the stockade, had been charged with mutiny and confronted with a court-martial.

Standing on the platform inside the campus plaza, the graduate student who was talking loomed above us. He spoke with edgy intensity, letting his utterances fall into a pattern of rat-tat-

74

tat words followed by abrupt, long pauses. He was followed by a young man who had served sixteen and a half months in military prison for refusing to carry a weapon or wear a uniform. His presentation was low-key, though his content was emotionally charged when he asked the spectators to identify themselves with the Presidio guards instead of the prisoners.

Now there was a bit of outdoor guerrilla theater, the military men attacking a victim (Pvt. Richard Bunch). The crowd commenced Pvt. Bunch's funeral procession, which would lead through the streets of the town adjoining the campus to the Selective Service headquarters. I found myself behind several students who wore chains made out of black crepe paper.

One, two, three, four ... Crunch, crunch, crunch, as our feet marched on the snow, Lord. A red traffic light at the corner, cars waiting, horns blowing. The procession was on its way. Local police provided color, rendering the event excitingly newsworthy for TV cameramen. "Why don't you get a bath and jobs?" shouted a businessman at the students in the procession. The long, winding column passed a downtown store window that held an immense flag-draped color photograph of Richard Nixon.

Women working in the Selective Service headquarters smiled and returned the "V" signs students were making with their fingers. The weather was colder now, as the wind increased in velocity. "Don't leave it on the sidewalk," a policeman told a group of students who were placing the mock coffin of Pvt. Richard Bunch in front of the entrance to the Selective Service headquarters. The students picked up the coffin, placed it on their shoulders, and resumed a clocklike marching procession up one side of the street, down the other, and back again. "Will you please cross at the corner?" asked a cop.

The agony of political helplessness was reflected in many drawn and somber faces of the college men and women. But why didn't more of the people in the town share the students' concern about justice, Jesus?

It is Christmas Eve, Lord.

Outside my window the afternoon light is fading. I'll sit here in the quiet for a few moments before I light the Christmas tree and turn on a lamp.

Other Christmas Eves crowd into my mind, and there is no room. How can I understand Christmas Eve, Jesus, underneath all the tinsel and loud music, the wrapping of presents, and pictures everywhere of you as a baby in a manger?

These next few hours, Lord—will I simply feel emptiness and longing? Will I try to cover them up with laughter and bright light? But I want to feel the deep meaning of this night.

Now it is growing darker outside, Jesus—in a moment I shall turn on the lights. Tell me, Lord, what was Christmas Eve like?

PRAYERS

IN A BLACK

STUDENT CENTER

"How do you see your role?" a black student asks me.

"I don't have a role," I reply. "I'm tired of all roles. I simply want to be myself. I don't want to wear a mask. I only want a face."

There is a ripple of laughter in the Black Student Center, Lord. I realize that it might be easier for me than for anybody else inside that room not to have a role to play. It is easier for me to claim anonymity in my whiteness. I have become the invisible man in a population explosion.

But how does my young black questioner see his role, Jesus?

"The only racists are blacks."

Seated inside the room filled with blacks except for myself, I recollect these words spoken by a white man two weeks earlier, Lord.

The white man had seen headlines and TV reports about black separatism, black rage, black self-determination and black nationalism. No one had explained to him why blacks were acting according to an unfamiliar script.

Wasn't integration the desired goal? I wished that he could hear the words of a black speaker inside the Center who said, "In the integration movement, whites controlled the traffic and selected the vehicles. They were half-stepping in double time."

In other words, Jesus, whites seemed to select a few blacks and then turn them into colored white men and women. It didn't work.

But I realize again, Lord, the wonderful irony of how deeply blacks and whites are brought together by mutually accepted separation in certain areas of life for the sake of liberation as a mutually accepted goal. This is sophisticated instead of simplistic. It demands a lot of honesty on the part of blacks and whites alike.

I become worried, Lord, by the dangers of isolation. Blacks need to understand the subtle changes taking place in that spectrum called "white opinion," as whites need to realize that they are not confronting a black monolith, but individual black people representing a complex of views.

Doesn't racism exist, Jesus, so long as we look at any other human being and see a racial mask instead of a human face?

Black isn't chic anymore, is it, Jesus?

I mean, whites no longer define it as glamorous, "now," or "in." The college men and women in this Black Student Center are on the whole pleased by their drop from fashion, Lord. They want to take care of serious business. Unlike their parents, they have entered into black awareness without an internal struggle. They're interested in getting an education and a solid piece of the action for black people.

Whites are welcomed to the Center if they wish to come. Their embarrassment or uptightness is seen by the black students as important in teaching whites what it has long been like to be black inside a white world with white institutions.

The Center is a remodeled house on the edge of the campus. There is a library of books about the black experience, an office for Afro-American Studies, a social room and a basement hall for lectures or dancing.

Looking at me, the black students' faces are quizzical but not unfriendly. I am received with open courtesy and frank talk. One particularly militant student says that he hopes I will not misconstrue his lack of warm pretense as a sign of belligerence.

What is happening in the Black Student Center gives me hope for all of us, Jesus.

"A White Man's Heaven Is a Black Man's Hell."

I heard this song many, many times when it was sung by young black nationalists in rural Mississippi and Alabama during civil-rights demonstrations in the early sixties. Would these black students, seated in their Center, sing it too?

Yes, I suppose so, Lord. At least they would think it. For their experience of human life has been very hemmed in by white power, hasn't it, Jesus? I imagine they dream of getting away, even just once, from white judgments, ways of doing things, and ingrained attitudes toward black people.

This must be why, Lord, an occasional black professor is such a welcome change from a white one. And a black administrator, a black judge, a black journalist, a black TV personality, a black priest and a black mayor.

A white man's heaven. It would be hell in its isolation, wouldn't it, Jesus?

Would genocide against blacks be possible, Jesus?

I watch black fury on the one hand, and white nonunderstanding of it, coupled with fear and angry hurt, on the other.

White ignorance about black experience in America now seems almost deliberate, Lord. Nor do whites know the actual conditions (around a corner in the city or across a town) in which blacks live day by day in second-, third- or fourth-class citizenship. I am talking not about the small middle class but about the masses.

Whites and blacks do not know each other in relaxed, honest, open ways. They often meet in time-clock situations, and then the time runs out, the alarm clock goes off.

A black student at the Center mentions the question of genocide. It has a way of being asked. Perhaps the very recent death of six million Jews in Europe automatically demands its consideration.

Such genocide here seems impossible to me, Jesus. But then I remind myself that I am white. I forget the white genocide against Native Americans that happened here. There was the deep burst of feeling against Japanese-Americans in World War II. With its irrational fears and unconfessed sins, that happened here.

As a white, how can I help to make this question an unreal one? If I were black, would I consider genocide in America an impossibility, Lord?

Why do many people simply see violence in black and white, Lord?

I remember when a white student shouted to a black student during a demonstration on a campus: "Come on! We're going to burn the place down!" "No," said the black student. "I want an education. I want one for my brother and sister too."

Don't whites need to understand white consciousness, Jesus, as blacks need to understand black consciousness? In this way, both might come to comprehend human consciousness.

What is black consciousness, Lord? It seems to comprise many things—an understanding of what slavery did to men and women, soul music, Afro hair, African history, soul food, pride in identity, hip, a life style that differs from the white, survival under oppression, blackening the mind, and cool.

What is white consciousness, Lord? It seems to comprise many things—an understanding of what a feeling of superiority instead of equality did to men and women, European tradition, the legacy of puritanism, ethnic background, guilt, ownership of property, creating God in the likeness of a white man, the illusion of a master race, and success, with its nightmare companion, failure.

Tell us about human consciousness, Jesus.

"I don't want to live in a South Africa," a white student told me the other day.

He referred, Jesus, to the separatism between black and white students on his campus. According to him, the blacks eat alone at separate tables in the dining hall, do not always acknowledge a friendly greeting outside a classroom, limit relationships with whites to an absolute minimum of contact, and spend most of their time inside the Black Center.

The white student explained that he didn't feel he should be made to pay for the sins or failures in race relations of his grandparents or parents, Lord.

His comments reminded me of something a black student had said. "I'll refuse from now on to be a textbook for whites. If they want to know about blacks, they should learn it from books or their professors. On my own time, I need to study or be with friends to relax. I'm not going to teach a white kid with my life all the time."

Be with the black student, Lord, and be with the white student, and help each to understand the other's feelings.

**I feel so old when it comes to blacks and whites,
Jesus.**

I mean, I can remember only a few years ago
when blacks and whites could not eat together in a
public dining room or stay at the same hotel. Looking now at the black students surrounding me, I realize this is a part of their folklore or past history,
and does not concern their present experience.

I recollect a visit I paid to a university in the
South, Lord, several years ago. Whites and Negroes—as blacks were then called—were scattered
through the dining hall at a luncheon in my honor.
That is to say, people were not seated in rigid color
blocs. This seemed healthy and promising. But I
was wrong, Jesus.

Most of the whites and blacks present had never
laid eyes on each other before. Blacks were singu-
larly unwelcome here. The atmosphere could have
been cut with a very sharp knife. Nobody seemed
to breathe normally.

When this reality finally got through to me, I
tried to break the tension. I told a few of the ex-
tremely funny, warm and earthy stories that had
grown out of the civil-rights struggle, these seem-
ing to represent about the only really spontaneous
and present American humor still in existence. No
one laughed, Jesus.

Zeroing in, I told facts about second-class citizenship and the truth about the black experience in
white America. I thought it was time these people
heard about such things, especially as they were
seated in an integrated group that apparently
would not soon, if ever, be duplicated. Again,
breathing had stopped.

Inside that room, Lord, both the blacks and whites had been conditioned—for how long?—not to trust each other at all. They had been taught not to look at each other as human beings but only as "Negroes" and "whites." Later I was told that most whites seated in that room had been taught by their churches, newspapers, schools and families that civil-rights activists, and others involved in the racial struggle for justice, were indisputably members of the Communist party.

Many people have died for the cause of human liberation, Lord. Will it be won?

Black is not alien to me, Jesus.

It used to be. It was different, so I feared it.
White was supposed to be clean, pure and holy.
Black, I learned, was its opposite. Wasn't black a
coal pit of sin and a moonless night of death?

I saw a black face, Lord. It smiled at me. Then I
saw the Manichaean contrast of white teeth. I
could not smile back. Who was this strange crea-
ture who greeted me? What harm did he mean to
do to me? I had to ask myself, Lord, if he was human.

The first time I was alone as a white in a room
filled with black men and women I was disturbed,
Jesus. I tried to breathe evenly. What was expected
of me? I laughed, smiled, frowned, told jokes, and
sought emotional refuge.

Now I can discern black friendship, black anger,
black hurt, black love, black deceit, black rage and
black tenderness. These are human, Lord, and a
part of me.

Black is not alien to me, Jesus.

PRAYERS

FOR

LIBERATION

Why can't we permit the liberation of people and living things, Jesus?

Why can't we permit our own liberation?

"The universe has consciousness," the young Chicano told me.

"But the world is now uninhabitable. Man is acting fiercely against the consciousness of the universe."

It seems to me that we have a deadly definition of gods, Lord. We feel that to be a god is to ride roughshod over the earth, make decisions capriciously, act without feeling, and try to create terror in other people. We feel that to be a god is to claim the whole earth, and all of life within it, for our own use and destruction.

Could we start acting like humans, Jesus?

She feels that she has simply been programmed all of her life, Jesus.

What did it mean to be a woman? To her it meant an absence of equal opportunities, a sex role that became cloying, prescribed duties as a wife and a mother, social definitions of what she should legitimately feel and do in her life, rigidly imposed restrictions, contrasted with her husband's open sexual freedom outside their marriage, and a sense of dependence and powerlessness that has left her finally with a feeling of suppressed rage.

She is in her forties. She wants a freedom for the rest of her life that she has never known. She wants to break outside all categories that limit the full expression of her humanity.

How can she get outside the role she finds herself in, Jesus?

What is celebration, Jesus?

So many people call for props when they think of it—lights, candles, incense, robes. They call for a crowd of people—movement, density, bodies, choreography. They demand music. But aren't they performing, Lord? If they are playing roles, isn't it possible that celebration eludes them?

It seems to me that celebration is being free. Being one's own self, not trapped in a performance. Behaving naturally and letting one's weakness show, and being loved for oneself.

Power staggers my imagination, Jesus.

For example, Americans make up 6 percent of the world's population, yet America consumes 53 percent of the world's nonrenewable natural resources each year.

The United States nuclear arsenal contains 1,000 Minuteman missiles located within the country. Each one is equipped with a one-megaton warhead with from fifty to one hundred times the destructive power of the Hiroshima bomb.

The United States has dropped 180 pounds of bombs for every man, woman and child in both North and South Vietnam.

The United States has dropped 25 tons of bombs for every square mile of territory in both North and South Vietnam.

Is there a law of compensation for the uses of power, Jesus? I wonder how mercy and responsibility should be balanced with self-interest. I ask myself what security really means, Lord. Ultimately it seems to be concerned with living at peace in the world with other people.

Can we achieve that kind of security, Jesus?

A high-school student was talking to me, Jesus.

"I am a stranger to my parents," she said. "They treat me like a child instead of a human being. My mom can't be a friend, only a mother. All my parents do is judge. I don't think they realize how much they have hurt me."

Julie told me that she planned to move away from her family and start life on her own as soon as she reached the age of eighteen.

"I've tried harder than you know to communicate with my mom and dad," she continued. "They don't hear me. They don't understand what I tell them. I don't see why they can't unbend and be human. Lately I've given up trying. I'm just indifferent and don't say anything. I keep out of their way and stay out all the time except when I sleep. It's better this way. There's less friction."

Soon after this conversation I chatted with a parent who is the mother of three children.

"My children are all strangers to me," she said. "Oh, I mean partially, of course. I try to remember what it was like to be a teen-ager, but I can't. So I don't really know what is going on inside their minds. I have a fourteen-year-old girl who is experimenting with marijuana. She didn't tell me. I found out. I must say that I am terrified."

She took a cigarette out of her purse and lit it.

"I consider one of our sons more of a stranger than the others. I wish it were not so. Again, I am not completely serious. But, you see, I don't know where he spends his time. I don't understand his long hair, his politics, or, God help me, what he is doing in his sex life. He deliberately keeps secrets from his father and me. I want to love my three children. I do. They matter more to me than anything else in life except their father. But unfortunately, strangers they remain."

I think that a lot of children and a lot of parents would like to be liberated from being strangers to each other, Jesus. Can they be individuals and still manage to communicate a sense of belonging within a special relationship to each other?

Some parts of virtually everyone's life remain un-liberated, don't they, Lord?

So freedom is too often an abstract goal instead of a present reality. How can chains of ignorance and hypocrisy be cast off, Jesus? How can liberation begin inside countless individual bodies and souls, minds and personalities?

It seems that no one is a bystander in the struggle for liberation, Jesus.

She is not yet ten years old, Jesus.

She has been shunted from one rat-infested tenement home to another for as long as she can remember. Her childhood is filled with memories of clogged, dirty toilets, garbage piled up on cracked linoleum floors overrun by roaches, cold winter air hissing through cracks in walls and windows, rainwater pouring down from holes in ceilings, going through days with sucking hunger at the pit of her stomach, the absence of warm clothes, and the growing, gray monotony of beginning to understand what hopelessness is.

She would like to be liberated, Lord.

It sits there in its solitary horror, Lord.

It is a place supposed to house people who are called convicts. That often means poor people, Jesus, who find themselves caught without shining possibilities. When they are caught they have no hopeful way of defending themselves or spelling out to society what a creative second chance might mean.

So they are put here. At different times this place is a snake pit, a torture chamber for the body and mind, a triumphant exhibit of machine and system over men and women, and an obsolete social experiment created by a nation that does not care.

The theory is that if a person is caught, he's guilty, Lord. Cut him off like a dead limb. Turn him into a rotting vegetable. Teach him crimes that he never before dreamed of. Since he's an animal, put him in the jungle. Don't help him to get well, force him to sit it out. Punish, don't cure. Hurt him in a thousand ways, don't let him hold onto a remnant of dignity. Make him pay, don't redeem him. In time society can begin to resemble a rotting vegetable too, Jesus.

Can we tear down this house of horrors, Lord, and start building new lives?

Exploitation disturbs me, Jesus.

It treats all of us as objects. It bothers me most when it is very sincere, easily palatable and disarmingly seductive. So we are sorely tempted, Lord, to buy a product, a personality, a cause, a war, an idea, or even a religion.

Some people end up believing they are exploiting the rest of us for our own good. I wish, Jesus, that all of us would avoid playing God.

He's black and he wants to go to Africa, Lord.

It isn't that he wants to run away. He is trying to find himself. He feels that he cannot do this in a white world with white men, white women, white children, white values, white politics, white religion, white education, white humor, white movies, white television and white leaders.

He is looking for his roots, his past, and his very identity, Jesus. He believes that he would feel free among black people in a black nation.

What is the essence of black and white, Lord? What is their relation to the mystery of our being human?

My God, my God, why hast thou forsaken me?

There is a burst of machine-gun fire and a
scream of terror and pain. A hand grenade is hurled
into a hut—someone's home—and, moments later,
five people are dead and their home destroyed.
Someone's crying, Lord. He is being tortured. A
woman and her baby are shot down.

My God, my God, why hast thou forsaken me?

The rot and agony of dying are all around us.
Sadly, we have passively accepted it for so long
that now we can scarcely muster genuine indigna-
tion or tears. Death has come to mean an impersonal body count. The word has come to us, night
after night, day after day, within the sanctuaries of
our homes and over color-TV sets that make the
blood look as real as it does in Westerns. But the
human blood of young Americans and Vietnamese,
Latin Americans and Africans, Arabs and Israelis,
is not synthetic. Why—O God—must we tear open
human bodies and cause their blood to be shed and
drained into the earth?

My God, my God, why hast thou forsaken me?

The Nazi experience: it was only twenty-five
years ago. Six million Jews perished in genocide.
Organized religion accommodated the state and its
own secure position within society. Severe repres-
sion lashed out angrily and mercilessly at dissent.
The prophets? There were only a few of them. The
prophets? Let them be punished—tear out the
tongues that offended! Burn the hands that wrote
heresy against the state! Lash proud shoulders to
wash them in blood! Silence the prophets. Silence
them. Silence them.

104

My God, my God, why hast thou forsaken me?

We shall conquer the moon and space. We shall vanquish foreigners who seek self-determination and move against our wishes or national policy. We shall defend the power of the status quo against the rising aspirations of the young, poor people, black people, Chicanos, native American Indian people. Our future—is it written in plastic, in chrome, in dollars, in monumental waste, in guns, in nuclear overkill, in whiteness that is opposed to color, in respectability that breeds on personal salvation with indifference to the needs of others, in morality that is offended by the act of love but not the act of death?

My God, my God, why hast thou forsaken me?

We mark the death of Christ, the death of the world. We look ahead to the possibility of imprisoning life if we remain deadened to change, accept dumbly what is told us, and bury dissent and therefore democracy.

It is a time of self-examination, looking inward toward the conscience—and therefore out at the world; seeking to identify with the suffering and death of Jesus—as well as that of Christ within our brothers—in order to participate in resurrection.

JESUS

PRAYERS

I need to pray again, Jesus.

I grew tired of saying words that I couldn't seem to do anything about. It seemed hypocritical, Lord, to pray when I felt hopeless and sad. I didn't want to go on keeping you at a great distance, asking you to give me just what I thought that I wanted, as if you were magic.

Can't I simply let you be here with me and not ask you for anything? I just want to talk with you and be silent with you. Can't I love you and not use you, Jesus?

Who are you, Jesus?

Many pictures that I see portray you as a white man with blond hair and blue eyes.

A lot of people assume that you were celibate, yet the question has been raised as to whether or not you were married.

Some of us shut out every picture of your life except that of your activism. So you end up basically having an image of becoming angry inside the temple when you overturned the tables of the money changers.

Others of us see you only as quiet and contemplative, a walking example of the Twenty-third Psalm.

I would like to separate fantasy from reality in your life, Jesus.

Do you need me to act as your public-relations man, Jesus?

I don't think you do. I may work in your service, but your success doesn't depend upon my success. You do not fail if I am not effective. This frees me from a terrible slavery to myself under the guise of succeeding for you.

You are not mocked, Lord. Your kingdom has already come. It is established in human life. I can cooperate with it but can never usher it in.

Why do some people say it is necessary to win money, large numbers of converts, publicity and prestige for you? I believe this is a tragic snare and delusion, Lord. It has led to the church's fatal silence on issues where following you would have meant its own loss of these things.

Some Christians speak of the church as an army, Lord. You are presumably the general, and the army is supposed to fight valiantly for your victory in the world, even if it must sometimes kill, maim or pillage.

Is anyone, anywhere, ever meant to be manipulated, sacrificed or dehumanized for your success, Jesus?

A hard question for me is slowly taking formation,
Jesus.

Does participation in Christianity mean that a
person enjoys the understanding of other people?
Or does it imply estrangement, rejection and
misunderstanding?

I wonder if perhaps these are the last days of our
particular civilization and even the world as man
has known it. So can Christianity any longer be the
easy, comfortable thing it has seemed in the past
for those who never suffered because of their faith?
It has become acceptable to make religion a quiet
sanctuary in which the cries of the world's pain
cannot be heard.

It seems to me that being a Christian now will
increasingly involve your cross and many individual crosses, Lord. Maybe Christians will find they
can act only out of a sense of conscience and never
as participants in a popularity contest.

I ask myself if Christianity will become Christlike. Does anything else about it really matter,
Jesus?

You were an anti-hero of your own day, Jesus.

This seems important, because many people tell oppressed victims of society that they should accept things as they are. You are quoted, Jesus, as saying that some things belong to Caesar, or his duly constituted overseers, and other things belong to God.

But is there holy or human justification for unchanged order under establishment law, Jesus? It is claimed that you stand for reconciliation. I can understand this and agree with it. But reconciliation so often becomes subservience to the existing and unjust order instead of justice and change.

The victim of society's cruelty is supposed to be reconciled to his unchanged condition. Why isn't society supposed to be reconciled to the shattering of a false peace based on injustice, Lord?

Tell me about the Kingdom of God, Jesus.

In terms of my words and concepts, is it conservative, liberal, radical, revolutionary, left-wing, right-wing, none of these, a combination of them, or something altogether different?

I become confused, Lord, when some people claim their way is the sole way of knowing the kingdom. But aren't all of us imperfect in our motives and actions? That is, we tend to be ruthless in order to achieve change and satisfied with the status quo, satisfied with our methods for change and ruthless in preserving the status quo.

Is the Kingdom of God changing all of the time, Lord, or does it remain stable? In the Kingdom of God, what does "revolutionary" mean?

Do you want me to imitate you, Jesus?

I'm not at all sure that you do. I feel that you probably want me to become fully myself.

But if I wanted to imitate you, Jesus, how could I do it? You were raised in the Jewish religious tradition of your time, I in the Christian religious tradition of my time and place. You lived in a rural, primitive society, while I live in an urban and sophisticated one. You dwelt under Roman occupation, while I live in the Rome of today as a full citizen. You died on the cross, but today there are only gas chambers, electric chairs and hangmen's nooses. You lived in a world of limited communication between people, while I am surrounded by television, jet planes and teletypes.

But I realize that imitating you, Jesus, doesn't have very much to do with such things as these. It really means imitating your love, your honesty and your commitment, doesn't it?

Even when the church seems remote and cold, I feel that you are very close to me, Jesus. You are not a distant savior. You are here with me, transforming emptiness into fullness, nothingness into meaning, impersonality into identity.

I want to imitate you, Jesus. Help me.

Many of your words seem to be absurd, Jesus.

I mean, they are by the standards of society. You said that the meek will inherit the earth. Men who are reviled and persecuted for your sake are blessed. The kingdom belongs to the poor.

I am reminded of the Theater of the Absurd, Lord, and its use of paradox, poetry and myth to speak about life. It occurs to me that our ways of speaking about the truths of Christianity should be the same. Instead they are sometimes literal, fundamentalistic and dogmatic. Perhaps Christianity ought to be called the Faith of the Absurd.

It is certainly contrary to reason, Lord, to exalt valleys, say that the first shall be last and the last shall be first, turn water into wine, raise Lazarus from his tomb, announce that the Kingdom of God is in the midst of human life, die between two thieves on a garbage heap, and refuse to remain dead.

Isn't the absurdity of holiness the closest thing to its essential truth and purity, Jesus?

I want to be with you, Jesus, and I don't want to be.

Sometimes I feel that if you would just go away and leave me alone, I could make it. I mean, I could strike a neat balance between involvement and personal security. I could have some things my way, you could have some things your way, and I would very religiously and faithfully make the decision.

There are moments when I must ask myself the question, What do you want of me, Lord? I am generally a decent sort, basically loving, outgoing, respectable, hardworking, unself-righteous, generous and steady.

Do you want my heart, Lord? Do you want my mind, Lord? Do you want my soul, Lord?

I find it very hard to give them to you. Please don't quit fighting me, Jesus.

TWO SEMINARIANS:

A DIALOGUE-PRAYER

FOR THE CHURCH

JOHN:

I'm packed.
   I'll be ready to go after chapel and breakfast in
      the morning.
   It will be strange not to be here.
   I'm a stranger to the man I was.
Bill and I entered the seminary together.
   We were giving our lives to the church.
   What were we like three years ago?
   Bill has changed as much as I have.
   He's staying here.
   It isn't simply staying or leaving that is impor-
      tant, but what's honest for a man to do.
My life has never been so right as it is now.
   There's the feeling of a clean line about it.
   Tomorrow. Tomorrow morning I'll leave.

BILL:

My world, it's been shaken to its foundations.
   John didn't know what conflict he started in my
      life when he decided to leave.
   At first I thought I should go with him.
I've been critical of the same things.
   I've felt the same futility and hopelessness.
   Nothing *really* seems to change.
   This, despite changes.
   But afterward you look closely and see no
      changes.
The reason I'm not going with John is that I still

think there is hope working for change in the
church from the inside.

I believe in the foundations and essential structure of the church.

In the long run, John may do more by leaving the
seminary to preserve the essential structure of
the church than I'll do by staying.

Only time will tell.

JOHN:

I feel that I finally know who I am.

It isn't easy for me to leave the seminary.

I've put my whole life into this.

Future directions are hazy for me. There's no
easy road map to follow.

The alternatives are potentially cruel, but I'm no
longer so afraid of cruelty.

I'm more afraid of dishonesty, especially in myself.

It's honest for Bill to stay.

It's honest for me to go.

If I have to suffer some hardships now, I say yes to
it.

I acknowledge my needs as a man.

I can't think only about tomorrow.

I must be a whole man today.

BILL:

Yesterday. Today. Tomorrow.

How do these relate?

I respect the traditions of yesterday.

I want to live fully today.
I believe in the fulfillment of tomorrow.
Does this make me a conservative?
John places today ahead of yesterday and to-
morrow.
Is John a radical?
I think I can be a whole man working inside the
system
It just doesn't threaten my existence.
John forced me to make a free choice.
Stay or leave. Like that.
I'll stay.

JOHN:

After my first year in the seminary, I discovered
that I knew *everything* about God.
He was omnipotent.
He was omnipresent.
He was omniscient.
He was *He*.
Onward, Christian Soldiers.

BILL:

They taught me never to be angry or lose my tem-
per.
To love everybody, being available to all people
at all times.
To be Christlike.
To pray more than other people.
Some of my teachers said the church was not involved in the sinful world, such as
real estate

ward politics
racism
war
No.
It was holy.

John:

A clergyman will
conduct public worship.
minister to the sick and dying.
baptize babies.
marry men and women.
bury people.
Will a clergyman
march on a picket line?
preach a disturbingly honest sermon?
knowingly lose money for the church by telling
the truth?
protest actively against institutional racism?
stand publicly against war and warfare?
go to jail for his religious convictions?
feel lonely?
fight inside the system to change the system?

Bill:

It was during our first year in the seminary.
John and I both felt totally inadequate to be
here.
We felt sinful because we didn't love God
enough.

We wanted the drives within us for education
and a better world to become more holy.
John and I decided to pray together.
On two nights a week we set our alarm clocks for
2 A.M.
We met in the chapel.
We knelt down on the stone floor.
We prayed silently.
Once we prostrated our bodies, in the form of
Christ hanging on the cross, on the stone floor
of the chapel.
Body of Christ, save us.
Blood of Christ, inebriate us.
Passion of Christ, strengthen us.

JOHN:

For an examination, we had to be able to list all
the books of the Old Testament in order.
I stayed up all night, cramming.
Genesis, Exodus, Leviticus,
Numbers, Deuteronomy, Joshua,
Judges, Ruth, I Samuel ...
Study the prophets.
But don't recognize one sitting in the room with
you.
He might rock the boat.
He might upset the status quo.
Study church history but don't make it.

BILL:

The difference a few men made.
The right time and the right place.

John XXIII.
>He changed the church.
>He destroyed the Catholic world.
>He destroyed the Protestant world.

Bonhoeffer.
>He forced me out of the religious ghetto into the whole world.
>Religionless Christianity.
>I'm glad I am living now.
>I can stay in the system.
>I can help change the system.

JOHN:

The French worker-priests.
>They wanted to be close to people.
>They didn't want any separation between their lives and the real lives of ordinary people.
>They wanted the church to stand with the poor, not the privileged against the poor.

The establishment tried to break them.
>It failed, although the movement seemed to die or go underground when it was outlawed.
>*Unless a grain of wheat falls into the earth and dies, it remains alone; but if it dies, it bears much fruit.*

I feel a close kinship to these worker-priests.
>My interpretation of them is one reason I'm leaving.
>I want to work as a Christian with people's secular concerns.
>I don't want to spend my life and energy battling the establishment.
>Can I bypass it and be a Christian in the world?

BILL:

Why was I born into *this* age?
  Nothing can be the same as it was.
  Old forms don't give new meaning to this gener-
    ation.
I love old forms.
  To worship before an ancient altar.
  To wear bright vestments.
  To hear the Eucharist sung very, very well.
  I love these things.
  I find them exhilarating and meaningful.
This doesn't mean God is only *here*.
  It means, at its best, that God is here and there-
    fore everywhere in his world.
  But this is an age of pragmatism.
  Mysticism must, it seems, be found in involve-
    ment in the world.
I shall stay in the church and try to build bridges
    to the world outside it.
  John and I will have such a bridge.

JOHN:

For I was hungry and you gave me no food.
I was thirsty and you gave me no drink.
I was a stranger and you did not welcome me.
Naked and you did not clothe me.
Sick and in prison and you did not visit me.
  I'll try to be with Jesus in the world.
  I'll end up working with people, without a collar
    or a portfolio.
  Without the church's ordination.

127

I say yes to this.
As Jesus is in me, I'll be a priest of his.
Social action instead of organized religious activity.
Prayer actions in the place of mere prayer words.
Lord of life instead of Lord of the church.
Liturgy as action in life, not actions in ritual.
I am whole.
I want to be a man for God, in the midst of life.

BILL:

I am whole.
I'll be a juggler, like John.
Like John, I'll try to be a fool for Christ's sake.
There will never again be a neat, ordered pattern for me.
I can only try to follow Jesus' way of life.
I'll try to do this within the church and the world.
To see through the stained-glass windows.
To see Jesus in people's lives.
To see Jesus resurrected from religious forms as well as death.
To understand resurrection as freedom.
Not license.
Freedom.
I'll be busy.
John, my brother, what *is* priesthood?
We can try to find out and share it.

PRAYERS

IN

STRUGGLE

Don't crush me.

The walls are shifting slowly, easing toward me; they are liquid yet still contain form, like a wave. Only they move very, very slowly; smoothly and imperceptibly, Jesus. I must not cease my vigil for even a moment. The walls might crush me in a sudden, violent, single action.

Otherwise nothing seems to be happening, Lord. A deceptive calm has filled the room if not my life. A still life on the wall breathes gently. The patterns of a rug clash silently. A great colorful poster looks down, lifeless; how can it possess color if not life?

Ideas, like a rising wind, stir dangerously in my mind.

The walls have shifted again, rhythmically. Now they have come closer, Jesus. I rise to my feet, my powers tensed, and confront the walls. "Stand back!" I shout at the walls and whatever lies behind them. "Stand back!"

Isn't activism without involvement a delusion, Jesus?

I mean, wheels can be spinning. Ego needs can be met by ceaseless work. Guilt can be assuaged by self-righteousness. Everything can be organized on a big basis down to the least detail. But what if there is no involvement of feeling, Lord?

It worries me when activism is very romantic. Doesn't it become a form of escapism? Active people then seem to be locked inside smiling iron masks, performing good works on an automated assembly line. But it is antiseptic charity, Lord. People don't touch.

Don't good works have to get mixed up with blood, sweat and tears, Jesus?

I sit inside my jail, Jesus.

I constructed it with my own hands, stone upon stone, lock inside lock. Here I am a model prisoner of my own will. Here I am the slave of self.

Freedom is what I long for, Lord. My weary body and tired mind cry out for new life. My soul is parched and life is in decay, with dreams crumbled and energy stifled. Depression is heavy upon me. I feel hopeless in this moment, Jesus. I am only sorry for myself. I ask if there is any use to struggle with life.

But still I want a voice to cut through my silence, Jesus. Let me hear laughter. Let me see a burst of light.

I want to care again, Lord.

How machinelike can humans become, Lord?

It was a hot day. Driving down a hill, I could see the backs of a dozen or more cars ahead. Their rear lights would flash on—red! click!—then a few feet farther they would turn off. Now on again—red! click!—off. On. Off. On. Off. On Off. Fifty times going down the winding hill road.

My lights were doing the same thing, Jesus, as I placed my foot on the brake and took it off. On. Off. Was I operating the machine or was it really operating me? Everybody else looked funny, I thought, sitting inside the plain or brightly colored machines they were driving.

A lot of machines and people seemed to look alike. I mean, the appearances of the people seemed to fit the personalities of the cars they had selected. Did I look like my car? I may even have behaved like it. A question formed in my mind, Lord. Why do machines sometimes behave like the worst humans, and humans like the worst machines?

I have tried not to live an insular life, Jesus.

But it has been hard. A white, middle-class American is so marked in the world. He is a Roman with his power and money. I mean, I have never known what it really feels like to be Spanish or Turkish or Brazilian.

Of course, I have never known how it feels to be black. I have wanted to get inside a black skin, crawl behind a black face and look out through those eyes at myself. I never could. I could only look through my own eyes at black skin, Afro hair, and growing rage.

Which are faces, Jesus, and which are masks? Identities are so often mysteries. There are moments, Lord, when I wonder if I have ever known how it feels to be myself.

I wish that I knew what to do with memories, Lord.

Some things that I remember are too painful for me to bear. I try to hide them underneath layers of other thoughts. I try to keep busy so that I won't have time to think about them.

But at an unexpected moment in the middle of the day the memories and I are alone. They are remembrances of people I loved who are no longer here with me. They are thoughts about what might have been, Jesus. I wish that I had acted differently about many things. I can see how I took the wrong turning in this road and that path. Why didn't I understand how a blow to my pride was justified, Lord? I couldn't seem to see my life in an intelligent perspective and make the right choices.

What can I do with my life, Jesus, so that I can live in peace with memories?

Prayer for someone grieving after the death of a loved one.

I come to you at this moment in hope instead of sadness: that your burden of loss will be taken away, your grief transformed into deep faith and quiet peace, and your eyes focused in wonder upon the mystery and joy that the future holds for you.

My hope for you is that the love of the universe will be showered upon you, and you will be thankful and glad. Reach out your hand; take the freely offered gift of love.

He seemed to be a close friend, Lord.

Now I feel that he is a distant stranger. We are not communicating with each other at all.

Was I wrong before, Jesus? Am I wrong now?

It had always seemed to me that he and I looked at things in the same way. I felt that he knew my thoughts and ideas without my having to spell them out. I believed that I knew his.

Suddenly my friend's face became an alien mask. His ideas disturbed me. I could not share them at all. He expected me to do something that I could not do if I were to remain myself.

So a gulf has come between us, Lord. We are no longer friends. If we avoid contact, can we stop short of becoming enemies?

It makes me wonder what friendship really means, Jesus. Can my friend and I bridge the gulf that has grown between us? How can we do it, Lord?

I believe that terror is evil, Jesus.

Sometimes I am tempted to use it when I angrily protest against the terrorism of the status quo. An eye for an eye. A tooth for a tooth. Injustice for injustice. A life for a life.

But if one became a Nazi to defeat Nazism, wasn't he already defeated, Lord? I mean, he had become his enemy. He had allowed his enemy to win.

Murder doesn't win people's hearts. Burning, exploding and destroying don't make people love. "Love" is a misused word, isn't it, Jesus? Some people think it is soft to love. I don't think so. I believe that love can overcome hate. I believe that it can overcome terrorism. But why haven't we ever tried it?

How can I change anything, Lord?

Sometimes I wonder if many people hate too much for there to be any peace or creative change. How much time is left for humans to learn how to love?

A drug addict who said he was a philosopher told me to flee, Lord. He said terrorism is coming. He felt that idealistic people who had exposed their views had to stay out of sight and hidden inside the forests or else had to leave the country.

I am told by some young friends living in communes that a new Dark Age is coming. And that the only way to preserve human values is to nurture them in cocoon-like small communities until the evil has passed. Are they right when they say Armageddon is coming, Lord?

I ask myself if the best way to bring about change is to stay in the heat of battle, with the risk of heightening violence and the possibility of holocaust, or withdraw in silent witness. Should people strike out for survival instead of leading an open, risky life, Jesus?

Time is raging inside me, Jesus.

It is draining me of life. Each second is cruelly racing away from me. An hour seems a monstrous thing beyond my imagination, Lord.

I mean, will life itself be safe? There are so many dangers that threaten it. It seems the ultimate barbarism to destroy it. But the very threat makes it an indescribably rare gift. I cannot take it for granted, Jesus, or waste my life as if it were part of an unlimited supply.

I become frightened. How can I stop this flood of time? I want to shore up the moments.

But please do not calm my desperation. Do not provide any release from my aching fear. For I want to feel alive, commune with nature, and behold wonder through my eyes. I want to touch warm flesh, sense the depth of mystery, and ache with love. I want to perceive what is glowing radiance, outpoured kindness, and the rhythm of delight.

Teach me what life really means, Lord, and how not to waste it.